Koh Lanta

The Digital Nomads' Guide

Handbook for Digital Nomads,
Location Independent Workers, and
Connected Travelers in Thailand

By Barbara Riedel

ISBN: 9798879828085

Independently published

Table of Contents

About this guide

I am Barbara Riedel, and I have been living as a digital nomad since 2014. As a travel blogger, I have traveled all over the world in the last few years, always searching for places to work, information about internet (Wi-Fi or mobile) and so on. That's why I started a new category on my blog, Barbaralicious.com, called "digital nomad destinations." These blog posts contain general information for digital nomads that enable a smooth start in a new country.

After writing these digital nomad destination posts for a while, I realized something more detailed would be nice. I wrote my first Digital Nomads Guide about my second hometown – Palermo. I've chosen Koh Lanta for my twentyfirst guide because it's a famous hotspot for digital nomads in Thailand who prefer the beach over the mountains or people who want to flee from the burning season in Chiang Mai! And to be honest with you: Koh Lanta has a special place in my heart because this is where I decided that I really want to be a digital nomad back in 2015.

So... Are you looking for a beautiful island in Thailand with a great nomad community? Then Koh Lanta is the ideal place. It's really become a nomad hotspot, which is why Koh Lanta developed excellent amenities targeted for us laptop warriors. Prices will make it easy to live, even if it's definitely pricier than Chiang Mai, and you will not have any problems getting by with English – although knowing a little Thai never hurts. With few language barriers, a great community, and low cost of living, Koh Lanta might become your favorite island for your digital nomad adventure in Thailand. It definitely is mine!

Facts about Koh Lanta

Koh Lanta is an idyllic island located in the Andaman Sea. It's popular amongst digital nomads and young people in general for its possibility of enjoying tropical island life for relatively little money and since there are great coworking and even coliving opportunities.

It's a haven for travelers seeking a blend of serene beauty and cultural richness. Unlike Koh Phangan, which is famous for its Full Moon Parties, Koh Lanta is celebrated not for its party scene, but for its laid-back atmosphere and stunning natural landscapes. The island's charm lies in its tranquil beaches, crystal-clear waters, and lush tropical forests, making it a perfect retreat for those looking to escape the hustle and bustle of everyday life.

The island's allure is deeply rooted in its vibrant local culture and community, of which the Muslim community is a significant part. Koh Lanta is home to a substantial Muslim population, whose presence adds a unique and rich cultural layer to the island's tapestry. Visitors are often enchanted by the harmonious blend of Thai and Muslim cultures, reflected in the community's daily life, architecture, and culinary traditions.

Adventure seekers will find plenty to do as well. Koh Lanta's natural landscape is ideal for a variety of outdoor activities, from snorkeling and diving in its clear waters, exploring its coral reefs, to trekking through its dense jungles. The island also boasts some of the most beautiful sunsets in Thailand, best enjoyed on its pristine beaches.

In essence, Koh Lanta offers a diverse range of experiences – from cultural immersion and natural exploration to relaxation. It's a place where the beauty of nature meets the richness of Thai culture, all wrapped up in a relaxed and friendly island atmosphere.

Useful general information

Thai Visa Regulations

What Kinds of Visas does Thailand Offer?

Visa Exemption:

Thailand allows citizens of 52 countries to enter Thailand without prior documentation and for free. This means that you're visa exempt and can simply get in by getting a stamp in your passport. You can stay for 30 days. If you want to stay longer you either have to do a visa run or get a visa for another 30 days at immigration which costs you just 1,900 baht.

If your country is not one of the 52 countries that are exempt you will need to get a visa on arrival for 2,000 baht, which also allows you to stay for 30 days.

Single Entry Tourist Visa (SETV):

Another option is Single Entry Tourist Visa (SETV), which is valid for 60 days. You need to get this visa before your arrival to Thailand. You can get it in one of the countries surrounding Thailand if needed, but also in Thai consulates and embassies worldwide. In Georgetown, Malaysia many of the hostels and hotels offer a service to help you get the visa for an additional small fee. In Vietnam, the service is one day - drop off your paperwork in the morning and pick up your visa in the afternoon. Once given the visa, you need to activate it by traveling to Thailand within the next 3 months. There is an option of extending the visa for another 30 days for 1,900 baht and is not always guaranteed. Furthermore, many nationalities can now apply online.

Multiple Entry Tourist Visa (METV):

If you want to exit and enter Thailand again for six months you need a Multiple Entry Tourist Visa (METV). Then you can exit and enter the country as often as you wish as long as no visit lasts more than 60 days.

Education visa (ED):

If you're planning to learn Thai or are willing to take a Thai Boxing course you can apply for an Education Visa. Other options are studying English or enroll for a thai massage course. It allows you to stay for up to one year. Since the pandemic, prices for the ED-Visa increased massively, so if you like to move around and are not really passionate about attending a course for a few days per week it could be worth it to invest your money in visa runs and explore the countries around Thailand during your trip.

Visa Extensions

When your visa expires you have different options. One of which is an extension. You can only go for this option once if you're in Thailand on a visa exemption or on a regular tourist visa. If you want to extend your visa while in Koh Lanta you need to go to the immigration office in Krabi. It's recommended to go right before the opening time in the early morning or before the end of the lunch break. Better checking the exact opening times since they can change due to holidays, etc. You only need to bring the TM30 form (which you get from your landlord – just ask him, he knows!), your passport, a photocopy of your passport, a passport format photo of yourself, the visa extension form, and 1,900 baht. You can get the photo done by the officers or a copy shop nearby. They also make the photocopies for you. If you bring everything ready though you might be able to get the extension done in 20 minutes. If you're unlucky with the timing, the queues, etc. it can take up to three hours or they ask you to pick up your passport the next day. Bring a sweater if you're easily cold – usually the aircon is running in there.

Visa Runs

If you want to stay longer than your visa allows, your only option is to make a visa run by leaving the country, getting the departure stamp in your passport, and returning. Technically, you're allowed to return immediately after departure, as there's no requirement to stay outside the country for a certain period of time, at least not yet.

Even so, most combine a visa run with the pleasure of exploring a new place. The cheapest way to get out of the country is a ride to Penang, Malaysia. My husband and I decided on doing a border run in February 2024, which means that we left Thailand to come back immediately. We got a private driver for the day and paid 6,000 baht to drive to the border to Malaysia and go back to Koh Lanta the same day. There was an re-entrance fee for Thailand of 1,300 baht per person. So, in total, for two people we paid 8,600 baht to get another 30 days in Thailand.

A law has restricted the number of "visa-less entries" by land to two a year. You can come to Thailand as many times as you want by air on a visa exempt entry, as long as you never overstay your 30 days (or get the visa as an extension).

Currency, ATMs, Prices

The currency in Thailand is the Thai baht (THB). The exchange rate fluctuates constantly, but at the moment (February 2024), 36 baht are worth about 1 US Dollar.

ATMs are everywhere and almost all of them accept credit card withdrawals, typically with a fee. Most ATMs charge an additional 220 baht per withdrawal. If you are lucky the branch of a Thai bank office close by will withdraw money without the fee of 220 baht from your credit card bank account while just presenting your passport.

Another option is to open a Thai bank account. This way you can withdraw money for free and pay with a QR code which every local business including restaurants has. The only exception to this is 7-Eleven where they only accept credit cards and cash. I opened a bank account at Krungsri bank in Chiang Mai. They only wanted to see my passport with the visa (I was there on a regular tourist visa) and opened the account immediately and even issued my card. I can see everything in my app now and also use the app to pay with the QR code. It took me half an hour to open the account – 30 minutes, which made my life in Thailand much easier.

Typical prices are as follows:

→ 1l of water at a machine: 1 baht

→ 1,5l of water in a 7/11: 13 baht

→ 1 fruit juice in a café: from 70 baht

→ 1 fruit juice in a non-local café: 120 baht

→ 1 coffee in a café: from 60 baht

→ Meal in a local restaurant: from 80 baht

→ Meal in a non-local restaurant: from 150 baht

Transport

How to get to Koh Lanta?

By flight

Koh Lanta does not have its own airport. The closest airport is Krabi and you can find cheap domestic flights from several national airports. There are also international flights from and to Krabi airport like Penang and Kuala Lumpur, which makes it easy to get here. Check airline websites (like AirAsia) to find out if there are flights to Krabi from where you are.

From there, you have to take a van or a private car to Koh Lanta. The van will cost you around 400 baht. The private car will cost around 2,000 baht but is a big car and can be shared with many people.

By bus

You can also catch a bus, for example from Bangkok to Krabi. From there you have to take the van or private car as explained before.

By train

There are no trains going to this part of Thailand.

How to get around in Koh Lanta?

By foot

You can get around by foot in your neighborhood but if you want to go to different cafés, visit the waterfall or just explore the island, I don't think there's any better way than renting a scooter.

By Saleng

A saleng is a motorcycle with a covered sidecar. Since there is no local transportation like buses in Koh Lanta this is kind of the local taxi. They usually wait in front of the 7-Elevens or drive around and ask people who are walking if they need a ride. It is possible to get around by saleng. However, it can get quite expensive if you want to get around the island. A 5-minute ride can easily cost about as much as the scooter rental for one day.

Grab

Grab is the Asian version of Uber. Unfortunately, there is no Grab on Koh Lanta.

By scooter

You can and probably should rent a scooter or at least a bicycle to get around independently. A scooter costs around 250 baht per day, but you can usually get a much better deal if you book one for a week (200 baht/day) or even for a month.

In the last years, prices have risen dramatically in some areas. So don't be surprised if you're asked to pay 6,000 baht for a monthly scooter rental. You can still get much better deals but you might have to talk to many people to find one. One place that I know of where they don't rip people off is Time Travel Good.

Also, they try to keep your passport when you rent a scooter. This is actually forbidden by law so better ask for leaving a deposit and a passport copy.

On Thai islands, they have very few to no gas stations. You will find shelves with glass bottles and a yellow liquid in front of a lot of stores and restaurants. They are filled with gas – called namtaan in Thai. You can just stop anywhere and they even help you put gas in your scooter if you're new to this. It's usually 40 baht anywhere you go.

Beware of the fact that the rental is not insured and you're fully responsible for anything that happens. If you have insurance it will only cover if you have a motorbike license and wear a helmet. Most of the bikes in Thailand can't be driven with the regular driving license which means you need a motorbike license on top.

Internet

Wi-Fi

I definitely saw very fast Wi-Fi on Koh Lanta but it depends on where you are and what network you're using. At hostels and in resorts it's usually not the best. So, I can say that it's generally quite fast but it can also be unreliable in some places – if nothing else due to power outages, which can happen and sometimes last a while. In coworking spaces though, you'll usually be fine. I've tested

Wi-Fi speeds of around 350 for upload and 500 for download – and sometimes even more – and they have generators so you'll always have power there.

Mobile Internet

In Thailand, it's easy and inexpensive to get a local SIM card with data. When arriving, you will most likely find yourself in Bangkok's international airport, Suvarnabhumi. I would strongly advise you to buy your SIM as soon as you exit Arrivals. If you don't exit in Bangkok, just pick one up at the airport in Phuket, Krabi, or wherever you leave through. Although the sim cards at local stores are cheaper having a sim card will enable you to use Grab instead of a normal taxi to get from the airport to your accommodation. That alone might save you more money than the difference between the sim cards.

There are two main operators:

→ AIS

→ True

I always recommend getting AIS. They have the best coverage and you can add the so-called Super Wi-Fi to your normal data plan. The Super Wi-Fi allows you to get high speed internet all over Thailand through the AIS hotspots. To be fair, I haven't seen an AIS hotspot around Koh Lanta, but if you're traveling around Thailand for a while this might be a great option to have. And the Super

Wi-Fi is a kind of addon, which you can subscribe to on a monthly basis within the app.

You can also top up your sim card through the app of your carrier. Don't worry if you see that your card expires at some point. You simply top up your card and the expiration date will move forward. I usually make several top ups of 10 baht before leaving Thailand, which will extend the validity of 1 month every single time. So if I top up 10 baht 10 times I top up 100 baht in total to have 10 months more validity of my sim card. I then know that my sim card will still be working when I come back to Thailand.

Safety and Security

You will most likely feel safe on Koh Lanta and around Thailand, but there are a few typical scams and dangers you should try to avoid:

Credit Card Skimming at ATMs

Beware of scammers who clone your card to empty your bank account. The only solution is to be prepared with several credit cards ready – just in case! Always try to find ATMs inside banks or malls.

If you want to exchange cash, be careful not to get ripped off.

Pickpockets

Keep your valuables safe and be careful with bags. Don't leave your wallet, electronic devices or other goods in your motorbike case while bathing in a waterfall or swimming in the sea. If you come back there's a chance your valuables are taken by someone who opened the locker of your bike.

Traffic

Fatal traffic accidents are a common occurrence. It's mostly scooter drivers who overestimate their driving skills or the quality of the roads. Or both. When there is sand on the road it's easy to slip. Also, some people drive under the influence of drugs and/or alcohol. So please, be careful when driving your rental scooter and always wear a helmet and sturdy shoes, no matter how annoying they are.

Emergency contacts

In the terrible event that you need to contact emergency services, here are the numbers for your reference:

→ Fire: dial 199

→ Police: dial 191 (077 377 114)

→ Tourist Police: dial 1155 (this supersedes the old "1699" number)

Hospitals and doctors on Koh Lanta

Fingers crossed that you won't need a hospital but it's always good to know where to go if there's an emergency - just in case. Unfortunately, during my travels I had a few situations where I couldn't avoid going to the hospital, like when I had really bad food poisoning. On Koh Lanta, there are no hospitals but several clinics where they can help you whenever you need them. If you need a real hospital, unfortunately, you have to drive to Krabi.

→ In the North: TakeCare Doctor Lanta Clinic, 162 Sala Dan

→ In the West: TakeCare Medical Clinic, 533 Sala Dan

→ In the South: TakeCare Medical Clinic, 261 Koh Lanta Yai

→ In the East: First Lanta Jaylee Clinic, 16, 1, Koh Lanta Yai

Digital Nomad Groups for Koh Lanta

It's always nice to figure out stuff on your own, but sometimes we can do with a little bit of help. Luckily, there are some Facebook and nowadays also WhatsApp groups where we can find such help.

→ Koh Lanta Digital Nomads:

https://www.facebook.com/groups/KohLantaDigitalNomads/

→ Koh Lanta Consious Community:

https://www.facebook.com/groups/266173647369045/

→ Koh Lanta Expats and Regulars:

https://www.facebook.com/groups/1061216300638840/

→ Koh Lanta Rentals:

https://www.facebook.com/groups/koh.lanta.rentals/

→ Koh Lanta Nomads Whatsapp Chat:

https://chat.whatsapp.com/GyDzvPaacVeK8SwcKYxIFZ

Where to Work?

Coworking Spaces

Despite Koh Lanta being a small island, there are a few coworking spaces of which two also offer accommodation. These are your go-to places if you want to have fast and stable Wi-Fi and to work around like-minded people.

KoHub

*Photo from kohub.org

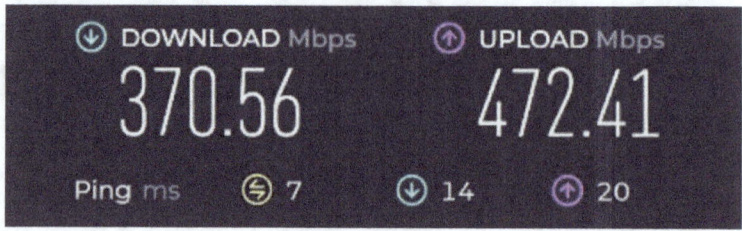

KoHub has already been here in 2014 and it became a real go to place for digital nomads traveling in Thailand. There is a wide range of options available to create your perfect work space. Join the community in the shared indoor rooms, rent a Skype booth or use the outside areas to hang out with the others, chill, or work while the restaurant is serving delicious food, coffee and tea. The space is open 24/7 but you have to check in before 5 PM if you have to register for a day pass or a membership. You will then get a password for the door to enter the space after 5 PM.

Prices: 400 baht/day, 2,000 baht/week or 6,500 baht/month

Address: 633 Sala Dan

Hours: 24/7 (but registration before 5 PM)

Website: kohub.org

Coliving: Yes

COWORX

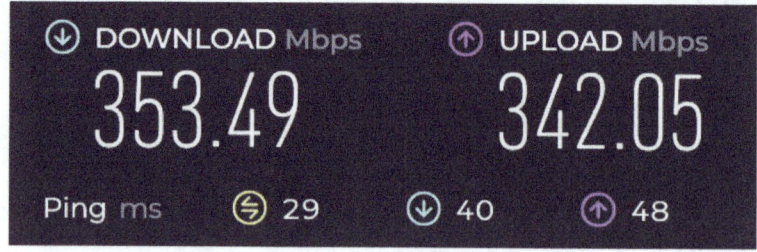

COWORX is a relatively new coworking space – it's been there since 2022. At the moment, they have six seats with fully height adjustable ergonomic office furniture in a quiet, relaxed and air conditioned surrounding. It's 2 minutes walking distance from the beach. Tin and Min are the two office dogs who doing a great job as guards of the place.

Prices: 240 baht/day, 1,100 baht/week, or 3,600 baht/month

Address: 272 Sala Dan

Hours: 24/7

Phone: +66 82 785 8674

Website: cowork-lanta.com

Coliving: Yes

Glass House Coworking

DOWNLOAD Mbps
56.62

UPLOAD Mbps
43.74

Ping ms   11   198   619

Located right at the mainstreet you can't really miss the Glass House. It's a mix of a restaurant, café, and coworking space with a tropical outside sitting area including a koi pond, and inside air-conditioned offices. In the membership, there is one drink per day included.

Prices: 200 baht/day, 1,050 baht/week, or 3,600 baht/month

Address: 85, 7, Sala Dan

Hours: daily, from 8:00 AM to 17:00 PM

Phone: +66 89 858 5957

Coliving: No

Cafés

I enjoyed checking out Koh Lanta's many great cafés when I wanted a change of environment. All the cafés I'm mentioning here I tested myself so you can be sure that they are laptop-friendly. In the past years, more and more cafés popped up that put signs that they don't want people working on their laptops. You can be sure though that in the cafés mentioned here you'll be very welcome. If you're running into problems, please, message me and I will change the book!

Hidden Hut Café

DOWNLOAD Mbps **131.61**

UPLOAD Mbps **129.29**

Ping ms ⑤ 16   ⊘ 192   ⊕ 80

Good coffee, sweet treats, all day breakfast and great lunch options specialized coffee place located close to Old Town. There is an inside air conditioned sitting area but also an outside sitting area on two levels. The food was not much but very tasty.

Prices:

Sandwich from 90 baht

Lunch dishes from 80 baht

Coffee / Tea from 60 baht

Pancakes / Waffles from 60 baht

Address: 267 Moo 1

Hours: Daily 8:00 AM. to 8:30 PM

Phone: +66 81 797 7321

Power Plugs: Yes

KHAOYAI Restaurant

DOWNLOAD Mbps
38.39

UPLOAD Mbps
25.75

Ping ms   ⊝ 25   ⊕ 104   ⊕ 317

KHAOYAI Restaurant is located close to Old Town on a hill overlooking the sea. This might be one of the most beautiful places here in Koh Lanta for me, especially since I like working with a view. The Wi-Fi was quite slow when I was working from here – but I guess you pay for the view, not for the internet.

Prices:

Seasonal fruit plate 185 baht

Fried rice with vegetables 125 baht

Egg sandwich 150 baht

Coffee / Tea from 50 baht

Fresh juices and shakes from 80 baht

Prices exclude 7 % service charge

Address: H359+2HQ

Hours: 9:00 AM to 8:00 PM

Phone: +66 75 697 244

Power Plugs: Yes, but only a few

View Point Restaurant

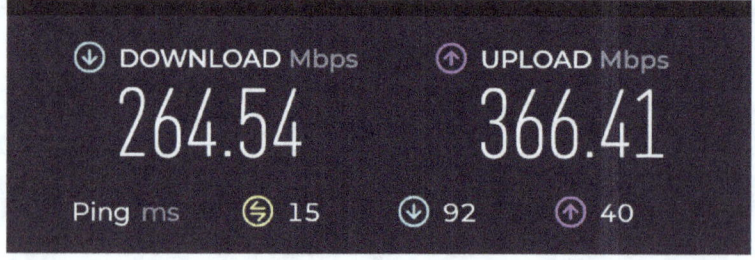

The View Point Restaurant is close to Old Town and basically right next to KHAOYAI restaurant. It really is a nice place, especially if you like working with a view. The Wi-Fi was fast and stable when I was working from here.

Prices:

Banana pancakes 90 baht

French Toast with butter and honey 90 baht

Yogurt with fruits and muesli 150 baht

Coffee / Tea from 30 baht

Fresh juices and shakes from 70 baht

Address: H359+8C4, 4245

Hours: 8:30 AM to 8:00 PM, Monday closed

Phone: +66 87 787 8697

Power Plugs: Yes, but only a few

Smoon

Smoon is located close to Klong Toab Beach. It's one of the best places for you if you prefer to work in an air conditioned room. The Wi-Fi is super fast and the food – even though it's expensive – is high quality and very good. There was no music playing while I was there.

Prices:

Soda Water 40 baht

Sandwich from 180 baht

Coffee from 60 baht

Fresh juice from 100 baht

Address: 241 Moo 8

Hours: 8:00 AM to 4:00 PM, Wed. closed

Phone: +66 62 563 9939

Power plugs: Yes

Living Room Bakery

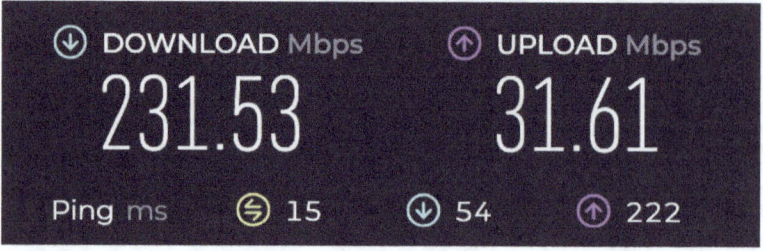

DOWNLOAD Mbps
231.53

UPLOAD Mbps
31.61

Ping ms   15   54   222

Living Room Bakery is located on the main street in Long Beach. It's one of the best places for you if you're looking for healthy breakfast options with Avocado, Eggs Benedict, or self-made bread and bakery goods. The Wi-Fi is quite fast and the food is expensive but high quality and very good. There is music playing so if you want a quiet space you have to create it with noise canceling headphones or go somewhere else to work.

Prices:

Soda Water 40 baht

Breakfast from 170 baht

Sandwich from 120 baht

Coffee from 60 baht

Fruit Shakes from 85 baht

Address: 692 Sala Dan

Hours: 8:00 AM to 4:00 PM

Phone: +66 89 466 1779

Power plugs: Only in the corners

What and Where to Eat?

Koh Lanta is a great place if you're a foodie. There are many local restaurants and lots of food options in general. One thing you have to keep in mind is that Koh Lanta is a Muslim island. Therefore, in most places, you will probably not find a lot of pork options except from ham (for example if you order a sandwich). For the rest, there are a lot of chicken options and also beef and being on an island, of course, fish and seafood.

Food

Koh Lanta feels like a pretty westernized place when it comes to food. Although you can obviously have Thai food and especially eat it at the night markets, there is no "typical or must-try dish" for this area.

Places to Eat

Street Food at the Night Markets

Night markets are not too popular in Koh Lanta. There is just one "nomadic" market that is moving around the island on a daily basis.

Local Restaurants

If you want to go for Thai food while in Koh Lanta check out the following places:

- Captain Bakery

- Jimmy's Fried Chicken

- Chef Chalong

- Ann's Easy Food

- Malina's Kitchen

- Lantas Café

- Coco Tango

Price for a meal: from 80 baht

Western Restaurants

Sometimes I just crave something Western. Do you know this feeling? And in Lanta, you won't have a problem satisfying your cravings at all. Favorites by digital nomads are:

- Cheeky Monkey

- Ohana Pizza

- Lanta Pizzeria

- KinBurger

- Yang Garden

- French Bakery Ko Lanta

Price for a meal: from 200 baht

Vegetarian and Vegan Restaurants

If you're vegan or vegetarian you will find lots of meat-free or even vegan options around. But unlike Koh Phangan it's not that you will find vegan restaurants at every corner.

- Fruit Tree Lodge & Coffee Shop

- Happy Veggie

- Habitat

- Aleena

Price for a plate: from 200 baht

Where to stay?

Koh Lanta can be broadly categorized into different areas: the north (Sala Dan and Kaw Kwang Beach), the east (Old Town), the south (Kantiang Bay), and the west (Long Beach and Klong Dao). Each area offers a unique experience, catering to different preferences and lifestyles.

Sala Dan, in the north, is the bustling heart of Koh Lanta. It's where most visitors first set foot, arriving by ferry. This area is a hub of activity, with a plethora of shops, restaurants, and markets. For those looking to stock up on essentials, there are several supermarkets and local stores. Saladan's vibrant atmosphere makes it a great starting point for exploring the island.

Just south of the pier, Kaw Kwang Beach offers a more relaxed vibe with its beautiful beaches and laid-back nightlife. This area is perfect for those who enjoy serene beach days and picturesque sunsets. While it's quieter than Sala Dan, Kaw Kwang Beach still offers a good selection of dining and accommodation options.

The east side of Koh Lanta, particularly the Old Town, presents a strong contrast to the island's beach-focused west. Here, visitors can immerse themselves in the island's history and culture. The Old Town is known for its charming stilted houses and quaint shops. It's a great place to experience a different side of island life, away from the typical beach scene.

Down south, Kantiang Bay is a gem for those seeking tranquility and natural beauty. This area is home to some of the island's most stunning beaches and luxury resorts. It's ideal for travelers looking for a peaceful retreat, with enough restaurants and bars for convenience but without the hustle and bustle of the busier areas.

On the west coast, Long Beach and Klong Dao are the epitome of the classic beach holiday. These areas are popular for their long stretches of sandy beaches, crystal-clear waters, and a wide range of accommodation options. From luxury resorts to budget bungalows, there's something for everyone. The west coast is also where you'll find a vibrant mix of beach bars, restaurants, and nightlife, perfect for those looking to enjoy Koh Lanta's social scene.

Each area of Koh Lanta offers its own unique charm and attractions, making the island a versatile destination that caters to a wide range of tastes and preferences. Whether you're looking for adventure, relaxation, culture, or nightlife, Koh Lanta has a place that's just right for you.

In general, I would look for two things:

→ Check if there's a 7-Eleven close. There are only nine on the whole island and it's nice to have one close.

→ Check if there's a mosque close to your accommodation. The prayers can be very loud and they put them on speakers no matter the time of the day. Our first accommodation was very close to a mosque and we were woken up three times every single night. We left after four nights because we were so sleep-deprived.

Airbnb

Airbnb is widely used in Koh Lanta. If you are looking for cheaper options or long-term rentals, the best strategy is to search for a place when you arrive as long as it isn't during high season starting from beginning of December. The peak months are January and February. Except from these busy months most of the places have long-term stay options on a monthly basis that are only available when you make an arrangement peer to peer or present yourself at reception. It's easiest if you do this after renting your own bike to make it easier to get around.

Hostels

Koh Lanta has many hostels. They are a great option for short-term stays if you want to connect with other travelers. They usually have slow Wi-Fi so it's really just to touch base from here with a budget solution while you're looking for a place to stay longer and check out the island to see which neighborhood fits your needs.

Resorts

Koh Lanta is filled with resorts – one next to the other. As with the hostels, they are better for short term stays. But, if you're looking to spend a lot of time chilling in a hammock, sipping cocktails, and getting massages, and only occasionally want to head over to your favorite café or coworking space, this is a nice option. Resorts I can recommend are:

- Blue Andaman

- Lanta New Beach Resort

- Popular Lanta Resort

- Isara Resort

- Lanta Lazy Days Bungalows

- Good Days Lanta Beach Resort

- Lanta Casuarina Beach Resort

Coliving Spaces

There are two coliving spaces in Koh Lanta: KoHub and COWORX. If you want to be surrounded by other online workers and have super-fast Wi-Fi this is the best option.

KoHub

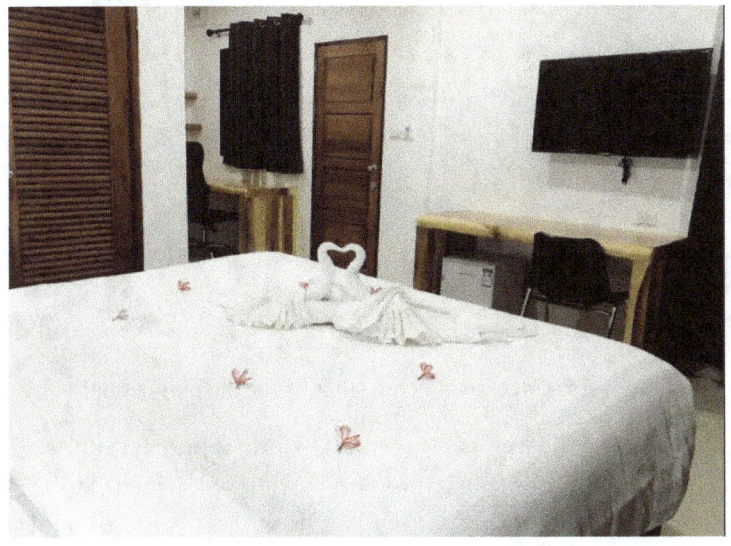

*Photo from kohub.org (thanks for the permission!)

KoHub's coliving prices start from 45,000 baht for one person for one month. There are two meals per day included as well as the one-month coworking pass at KoHub. You should be quick to book if you want to go in the high season.

COWORX

*Photo from coworx-lanta.com (thanks for the permission!)

COWORX's coliving prices start from 18,600 baht for a room for one month. There are soft drinks included as well as the coworking at COWORX. You should book about three months in advance if you want to go in the peak season.

What to see and do?

Koh Lanta is a tropical paradise and my favorite island in Thailand. But what's so special about it? Let's look into that:

Beaches on Koh Lanta

Koh Lanta is an ideal destination for those who love to witness stunning sunsets by the beach or enjoy a leisurely barefoot walk along the sandy shores. A personal favorite spot for many is the serene stretch of sand on the west of the island at Long Beach. Simply head towards Time for Lime or Lanta Animal Welfare and find a spot there. It's an exquisite beach for a stroll, especially during low tide when you can walk far out towards the horizon under the breathtaking sunsets.

Kantiang Bay boasts clear turquoise waters and soft white sands. It's perfect for those who enjoy swimming in crystal-clear waters. For a unique experience, visit the Old Town's eastern coast. While not known for traditional beaches, it offers a charming atmosphere and stunning sea views, perfect for a relaxed evening of dining by the water. Klong Dao Beach, on the other hand, is excellent for families or those who want to enjoy a beach day with all amenities close by.

Phra Ae Beach (Long Beach) is another popular choice, known for its lively yet laid-back vibe. It's a great place to enjoy a beach day with plenty of options for food and drinks. If you're seeking something more off the beaten path, venture to Nui Beach or Klong Jark Beach – smaller and more secluded, offering a peaceful retreat.

Koh Lanta's beaches each have their own unique charm, whether you're looking for a lively atmosphere, stunning natural beauty, or a quiet spot to relax. From the bustling shores of Long Beach to the tranquil hideaways, Koh Lanta's beaches cater to all preferences, ensuring a memorable beach experience for every visitor.

A Waterfall, Viewpoints, and the National Park

Koh Lanta is home to a wealth of natural beauty, with a waterfall and numerous lookouts scattered across the island's interior. A must-visit is the Khlong Chak Waterfall, located in the southern part of the island. The journey to the waterfall is an adventure in itself, involving a scenic 30-minute trek through the lush jungle. The path is well-marked and offers a glimpse into the island's rich flora and fauna.

For those looking for a more challenging hike, the Mai Kaew Cave offers an exciting adventure. It's a hidden gem located in the middle of the island, requiring a guided trek through the jungle and some climbing. The cave's interior is a spectacle of natural formations, with stalactites and stalagmites adorning its chambers.

The Mu Ko Lanta National Park, covering a significant part of the island's southern tip, is another destination not to be missed. It features well-maintained trails leading to breathtaking viewpoints, offering sweeping vistas of the Andaman Sea and the surrounding islands. The park's lighthouse is a popular spot, providing a picturesque setting for photos.

Each of these locations in Koh Lanta offers a unique perspective of the island's diverse landscape, from lush jungles and hidden caves to stunning coastal views. Whether you're an avid hiker or just looking for a peaceful spot to appreciate nature, Koh Lanta' is full of treasures waiting to be explored.

Day/Weekend Trips

Krabi

Embarking on a day or weekend trip to Krabi from Koh Lanta is an adventure that promises a blend of breathtaking scenery, cultural experiences, and aquatic adventures. The journey itself, whether by speedboat or ferry, offers stunning views of the Andaman Sea, dotted with picturesque islands. Upon arrival in Krabi, visitors can explore the vibrant Ao Nang Beach, a hub for shopping, dining, and beach activities. For those seeking a relaxed experience, the tranquil Railay Beach, accessible only by boat, offers a secluded paradise with its crystal-clear waters and dramatic cliffs. Adventure enthusiasts might opt for a kayaking trip through the mangroves or a snorkeling excursion around the nearby islands, such as Poda or Chicken Island, known for their abundant marine life and stunning coral reefs.

Phi Phi

A trip to the Phi Phi Islands from Koh Lanta is an unforgettable experience, immersing visitors in some of Thailand's most iconic and picturesque landscapes. The journey typically begins with a scenic boat ride, where the azure waters of the Andaman Sea and the stunning vistas of towering limestone cliffs set the stage for an exciting day ahead. Upon arrival at the Phi Phi Islands, the beauty of Maya Bay, made famous by the movie 'The Beach', is a common first stop. Although often bustling with tourists, its crystal-clear waters and white sandy beaches remain a sight to behold. Adventure seekers might opt for a hike up to the Phi Phi Viewpoint, offering breathtaking panoramic views of the islands. You should consider spending one or two nights there, especially if you like parties. Phi Phi is one of Thailand's top party islands.

Koh Lipe

A trip to the enchanting island of Koh Lipe from Koh Lanta offers a delightful escape into a tropical paradise. Again, the journey begins with a scenic boat ride. As you arrive in Koh Lipe, the island's charm is immediately apparent with its powdery white sand beaches and crystal-clear waters. The small island can be easily explored on foot or by long-tail boat, allowing visitors to experience its beauty from different perspectives. A visit to Pattaya Beach offers a vibrant atmosphere with a variety of beachfront cafes and bars, while the more serene Sunrise Beach is perfect for swimming and snorkeling, with its abundant marine life and coral reefs. For those interested in a unique snorkeling experience, a short boat trip to nearby islands such as Koh Adang and Koh Rawi provides an opportunity to explore untouched underwater worlds. The island's Walking Street is a hub of activity, where you can indulge in delicious local cuisine, shop for souvenirs, and immerse yourself in the laid-back island culture. As the day winds down, watching the sunset from Sunset Beach is a must-do, offering a tranquil and picturesque end to an idyllic day in Koh Lipe.

Useful Resources

Housing

- <u>Couchsurfing</u> (couchsurfing.com – free accommodation)

- <u>Airbnb</u> (airbnb.com – from cheap to expensive, rooms or entire houses)

- <u>Hostelworld or Hostelbookers</u> (hostelworld.com or hostelbookers.com – hostel booking platforms for cheap dorms around the world)

- <u>Tripadvisor</u> (Reviews for any activities and booking for housing)

- <u>Booking</u> (booking.com – hostel dorms, hotel rooms, etc. from cheap to expensive)

- <u>Trusted Housesitters</u> (trustedhousesitters.com – house and pet sitting platform)

- <u>Mind My House</u> (mindmyhouse.com – housesitting platform)

Travel Insurance

- <u>World Nomads</u> (Great travel insurance for short or long-term travels)

- True Traveller

- Safety Wings (a travel insurance from digital nomads for digital nomads)

Meeting Other Travelers or Locals

- Couchsurfing (couchsurfing.com – meetups, events and tours organized by locals and travelers)

- Meetup.com (meetup.com – meetups organized by locals)

- Internations (internations.org – network for expats around the world)

- Facebook Groups (Search for backpacking, solo traveling, group traveling, etc. Groups for your destination, e.g. "Backpacking Thailand")

Working on the Road (Work in Exchange for Food and Accommodation)

- Workaway (workaway.info – working for families, in hostels, etc.)

- HelpX (helpx.net – working for families, in hostels, etc.)

- Wwoofing (wwoofinternational.org – working on organic farms)

Platforms for Location-Independent Jobs

- Freelancer (freelancer.com)

- Upwork (upwork.com)

- Fiverr (fiverr.com)

- WeWorkRemotely (weworkremotely.com)

- RemoteOK (remoteok.io)

Flight Booking

- Skyscanner (skyscanner.com)

- Momondo (momondo.co.uk)

- Google Flights (google.de/flights)

- Kayak (kayak.com)

- Kiwi (kiwi.com)

Communication

- Skype (skype.com)

- Whats App (whatsapp.com)

- Telegram (telegram.org)

- Zoom (https://zoom.us/)

Safety Information

- Auswärtiges Amt

  (auswaertiges-amt.de/DE/Laenderinformationen/0
  1-Reisewarnungen-Liste_node.html)

- United States, Bureau of Consular Affairs

  (travel.state.gov/content/travel/en.html)

- Canada, Travel advice and advisories

  (travel.gc.ca/travelling/advisories)

- Australia, Smarttraveller

  (smartraveller.gov.au/Pages/default.aspx)

- Listing of Emergency Numbers by Country

  (en.wikipedia.org/wiki/List_of_emergency_teleph
  one_numbers)

Tools to learn a language

- <u>Duolingo</u> (duolingo.com – free tool)

- <u>Babbel</u> (babbel.com)

- <u>HelloTalk</u> (hellotalk.com)

- <u>Mondly</u> (https://app.mondly.com)

Practical Apps For Travelers

- Housing: Couchsurfing, Airbnb, HostelBookers, Hostelworld, Booking, TripAdvisor

- Transport & Orientation: Google Maps (download maps to use them offline), Uber, Grab, Rome2Rio (tells you all possibilities and approximate costs to get from A to B), Kayak, Skyscanner, Momondo, AirAsia, Ryanair

- Organization: Trello (to-do list and task management), Drive (online storage), Pocket (save articles to read offline later), Splitwise (Sharing the bill? Don't lose track about who has to pay what!), CamCard (scan a business card), Triposo (guides, maps, useful information about the place), Wallet (keep track of all your tickets), Google Photos (synchronize your photos and have an online backup)

- Networking for Travelers: NomadBase, BackpackR

- Health: Seven (7-minute workout), HeadSpace (guided meditation)

- Photo & Video: Foodie (for great food photography), Snapseed (photo editing app), iMovie (video editing app), VSCO (photo editing app), Lightroom (photo editing app)

- Other: SpeedTest (test the WiFi speed), NordVPN (secure your connection), WiFi Map Free (Searching for free WiFi? Get passwords here!), Currency (currency converter), Google Translate (download languages to use them offline)

The End

Thank you for downloading and reading The Koh Lanta Guide for Digital Nomads!

If you liked my guide and found some useful information, I would appreciate if you could leave a review on Amazon and follow me on my trips around Thailand and the world by hitting the follow or like button on my social media channel – @barbaralicious. If you go to places I recommend and you tag me on your Instagram I will share your posts and stories. I'm looking forward to seeing you living the digital nomad lifestyle to the fullest.

Always travel safely!

Barbara from Barbaralicious